The 7 Great Cities of Ancient Mesopotamia

Ancient History Books for Kids
Children's Ancient History

Speedy Publishing LLC

40 E. Main St. #1156

Newark, DE 19711

www.speedypublishing.com

Copyright 2017

All Rights reserved. No part of this book may be reproduced or used in any way or form or by any means whether electronic or mechanical, this means that you cannot record or photocopy any material ideas or tips that are provided in this book

In this book, we're going to talk about the amazing civilization of Ancient Mesopotamia. So, let's get right to it!

Euphrates River

WHERE WAS ANCIENT MESOPOTAMIA?

Ancient Mesopotamia has been called the "cradle of civilization," because archaeologists believe that the first cities on Earth developed there. The word Mesopotamia translates from the Greek and it means the kingdom "between two rivers." The two rivers refer to the Tigris River and the Euphrates River, which created a rich area of land called the "fertile crescent."

The land where Mesopotamia was located in southwest Asia is largely desert today, but thousands of years ago it was green and vibrant. The first people there were hunters and gatherers and there were abundant plants and animals they could eat to survive. The rivers provided fresh water to sustain life. Once people figured out how to farm and cultivate the land, the rivers provided the necessary irrigation to maintain crops and livestock.

Mesopotamia Plain

Bhagdad, Iraq

Today, the area where this ancient kingdom was located is now several Middle-Eastern countries. All of Iraq and

Iran

parts of Iran, as well as regions in Syria and Turkey, would be overlapped on a map showing Ancient Mesopotamia.

Ancient Farming

FROM NOMADIC TRIBES TO FARMS AND AGRICULTURE

The history of Mesopotamia begins with the history of farming. Around 8,000 BC, nomadic people figured out that if you planted a seed in the ground something amazing would happen. It would grow into a plant. This area of the world had many types of wild grains that could gradually be changed into crops and then farmed. This process is "domestication."

Wheat, barley, and lentils were three of the wild plants that Mesopotamian farmers cultivated. The same was true with animals. Many of the wild animals that were native to the area could be domesticated into farm livestock. Sheep, goats, cows, and pigs were all living wild in this area to begin with and then were domesticated to use for food and other products.

Wheat Fields

Nomads with their livestock

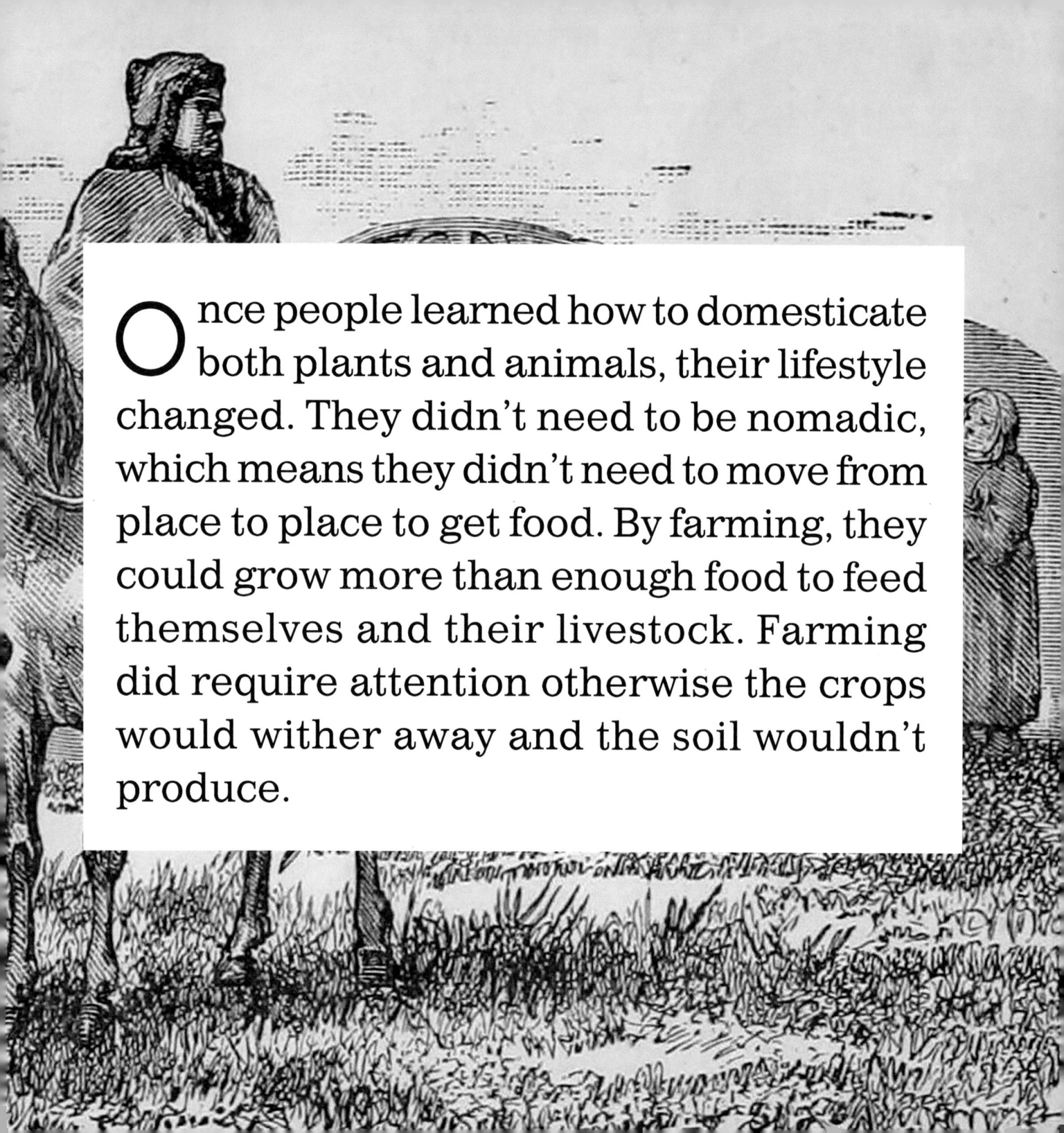

Once people learned how to domesticate both plants and animals, their lifestyle changed. They didn't need to be nomadic, which means they didn't need to move from place to place to get food. By farming, they could grow more than enough food to feed themselves and their livestock. Farming did require attention otherwise the crops would wither away and the soil wouldn't produce.

For the first time, people were staying in one place for long periods of time so they could take care of their farms. The groups of people who settled there needed the fresh water and fertile soil for farming. Mesopotamia was the first area of the world where villages and cities began to form.

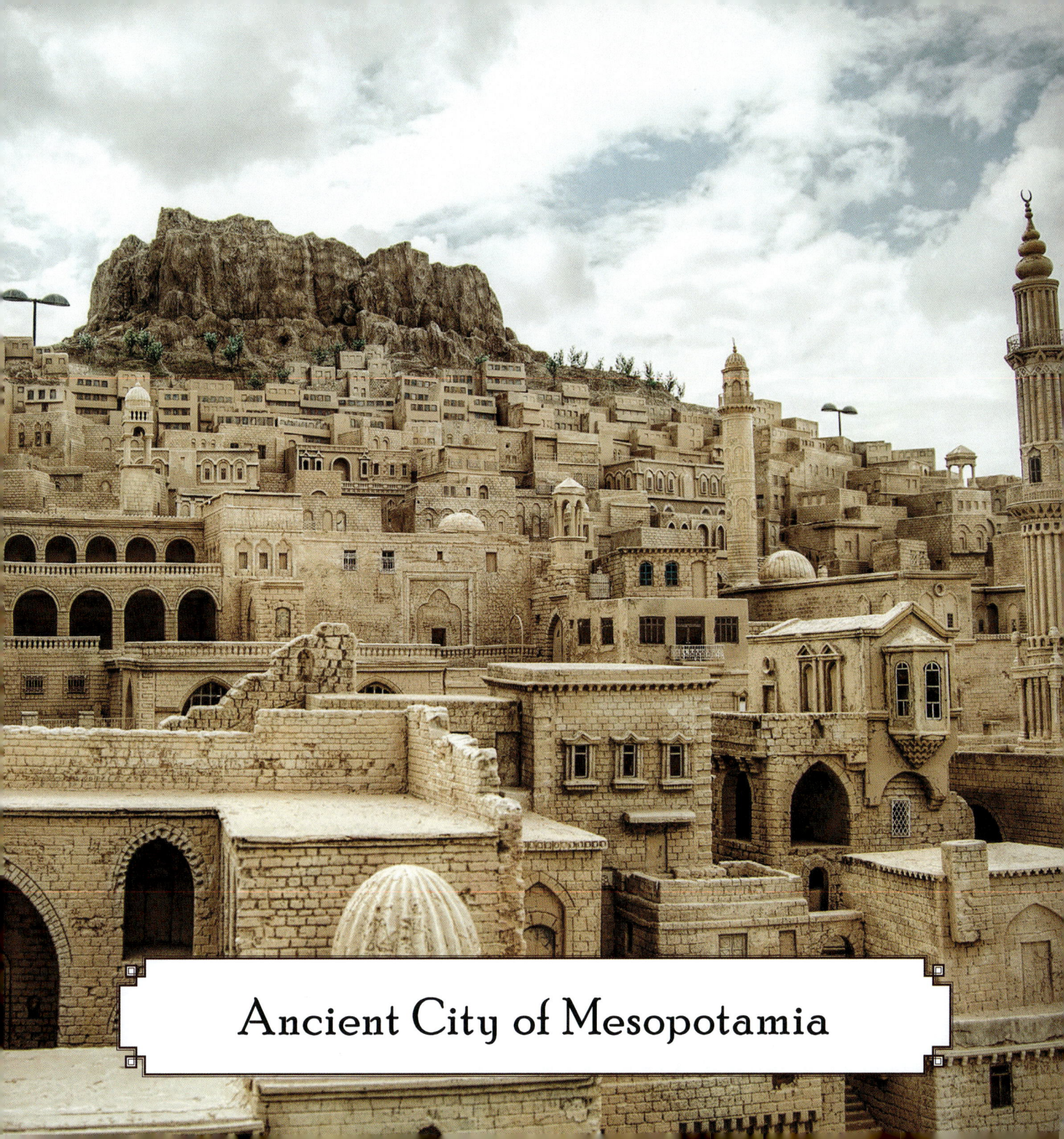

Ancient City of Mesopotamia

Cappadocian Houses

These first cities may have begun as early as 10,000 BC. However, a civilization doesn't form until there are some common cultural connections between the cities. Unlike the more unified cultures of Egypt and Greece, Mesopotamia was a "melting pot" of different cultures. Eventually, around 5,000 BC, the settlements developed into city-states with some cultural ties to each other.

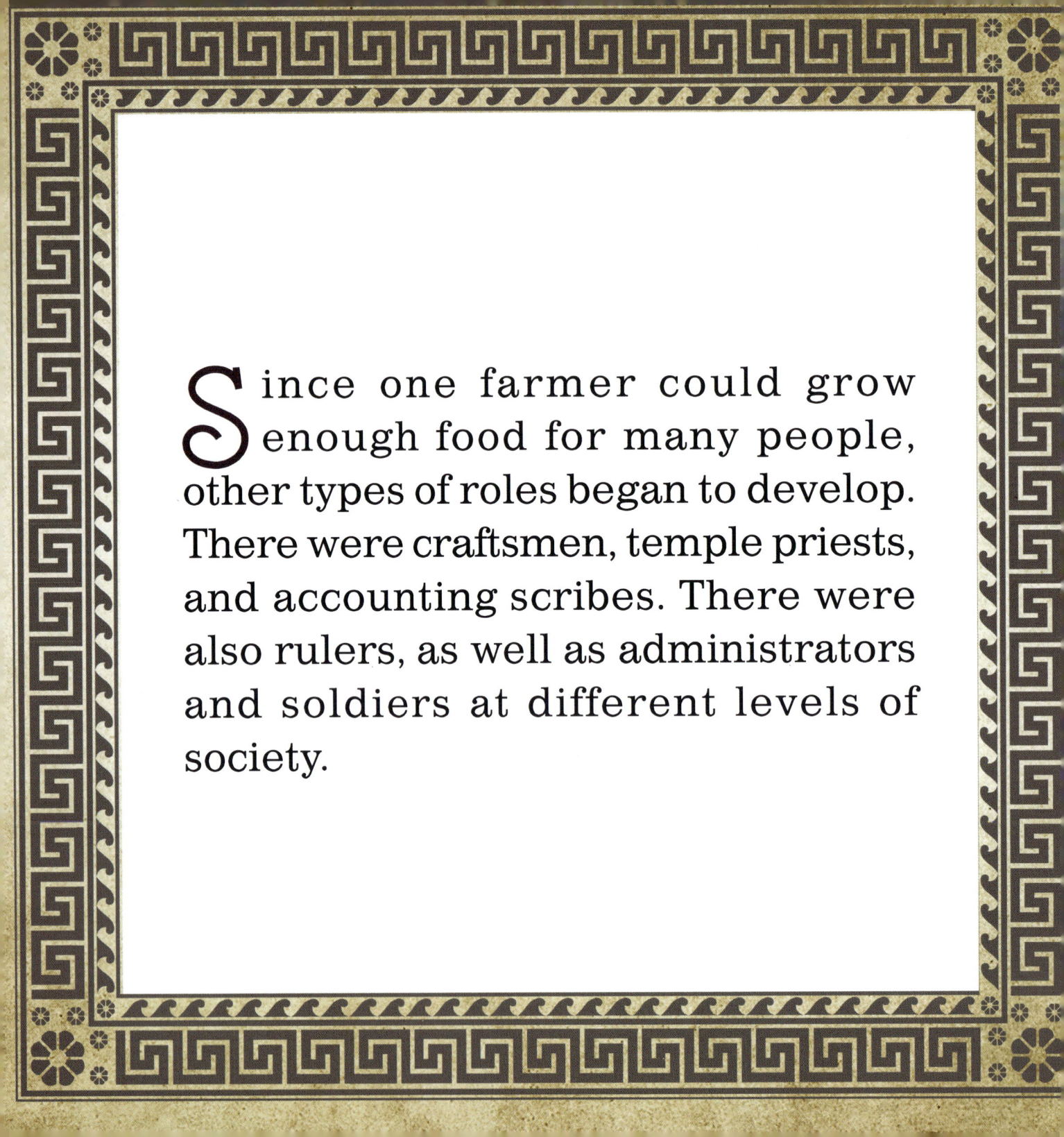

Since one farmer could grow enough food for many people, other types of roles began to develop. There were craftsmen, temple priests, and accounting scribes. There were also rulers, as well as administrators and soldiers at different levels of society.

Ancient Assyrian carvings

City of Babylon

COMMON CULTURAL CONNECTIONS

esopotamia was a collection of kingdoms, empires, and civilizations instead of a single unified civilization. Their thousands of gods were worshipped throughout the region although their names may have been different across regions.

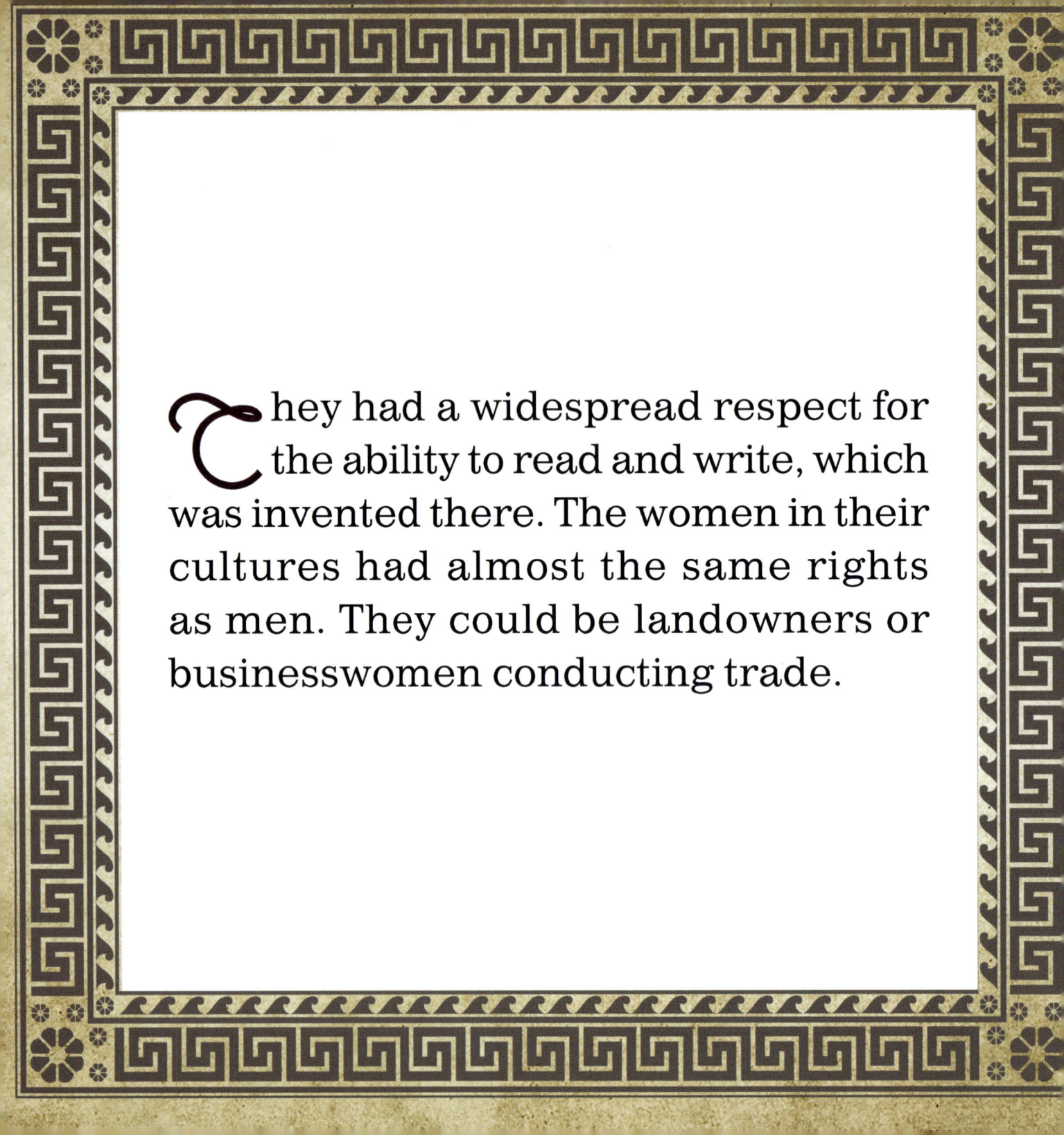

They had a widespread respect for the ability to read and write, which was invented there. The women in their cultures had almost the same rights as men. They could be landowners or businesswomen conducting trade.

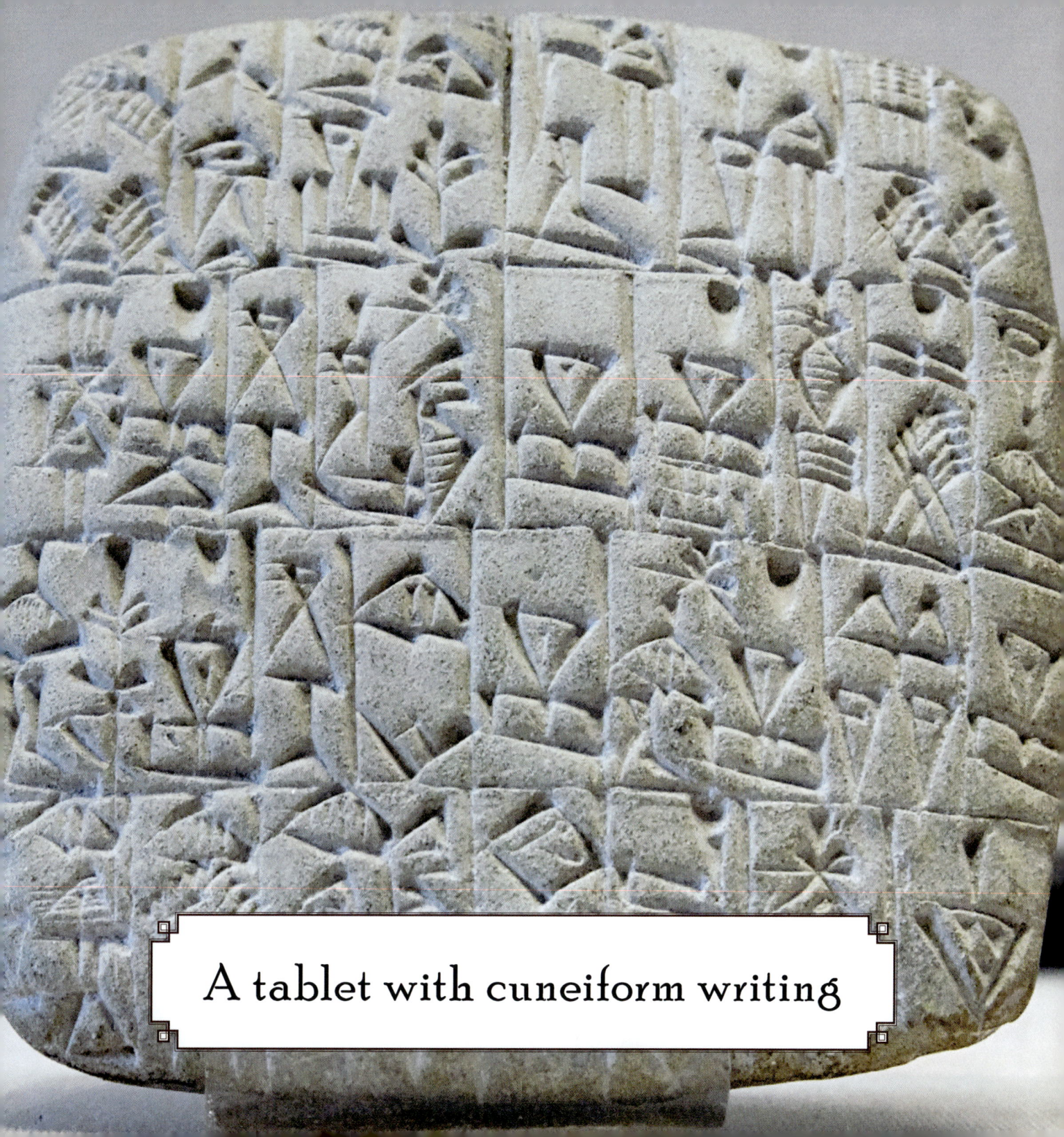
A tablet with cuneiform writing

Uruk City

URUK CITY

The city of Uruk was at the hub of the civilization of Sumer. During its golden age, around 2900 BC, there were almost 80,000 citizens there. At that time, it was the world's largest city. Uruk was started along the Euphrate's fertile riverbanks. As the farmers there perfected their agricultural and irrigation methods, they were able to grow large quantities of food. This made the city wealthy.

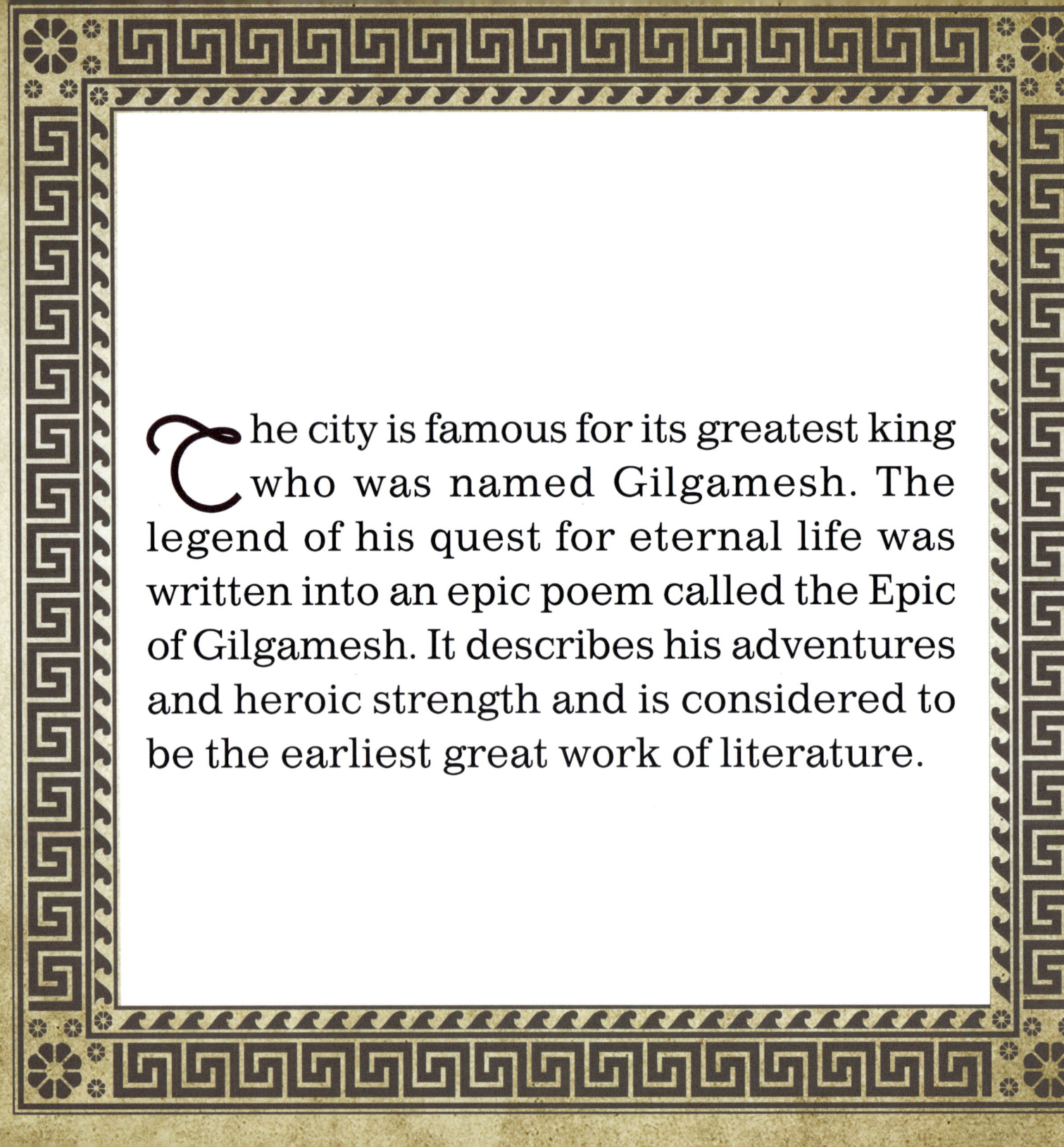

The city is famous for its greatest king who was named Gilgamesh. The legend of his quest for eternal life was written into an epic poem called the Epic of Gilgamesh. It describes his adventures and heroic strength and is considered to be the earliest great work of literature.

Gilgamesh Statue

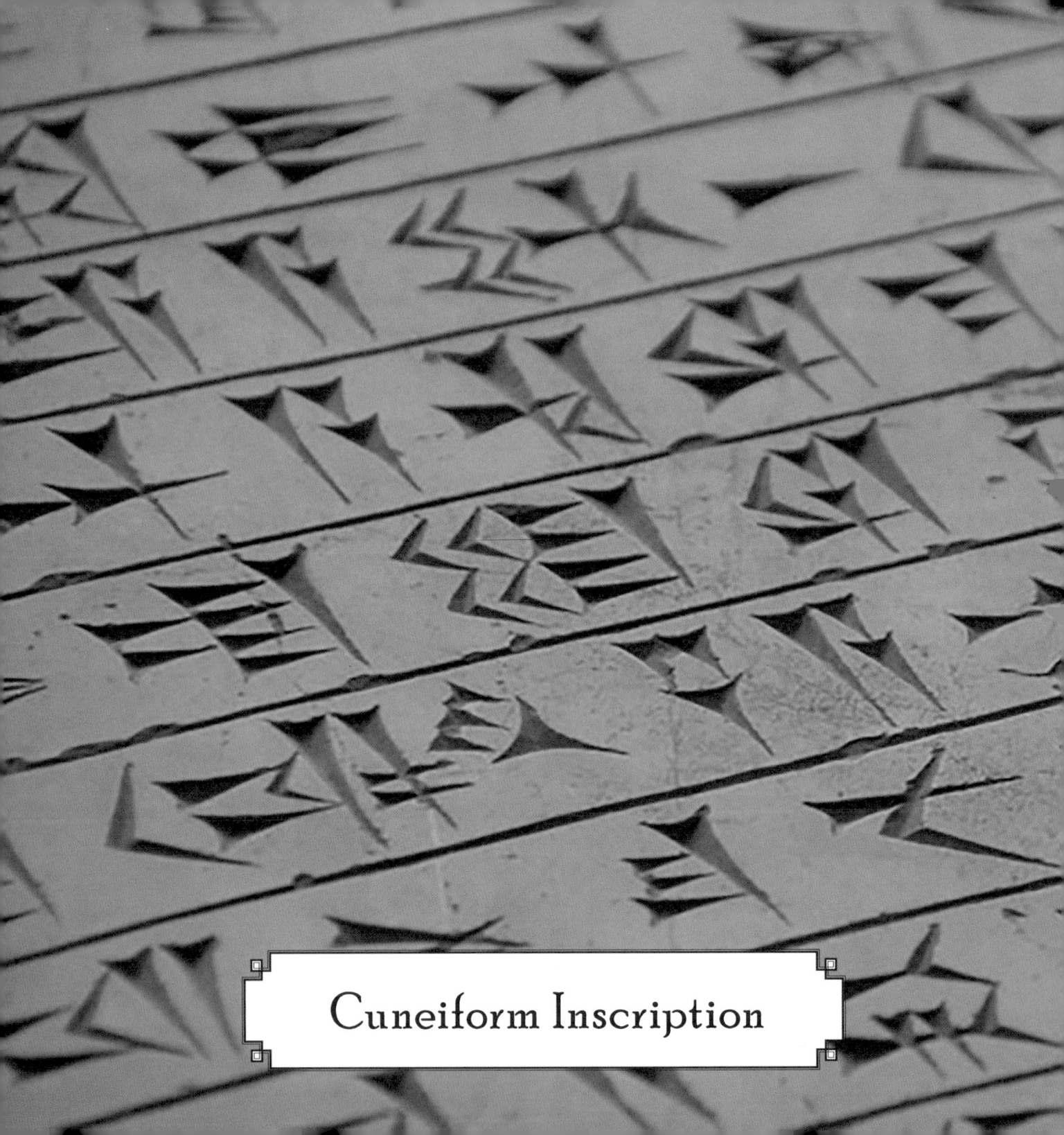

Cuneiform Inscription

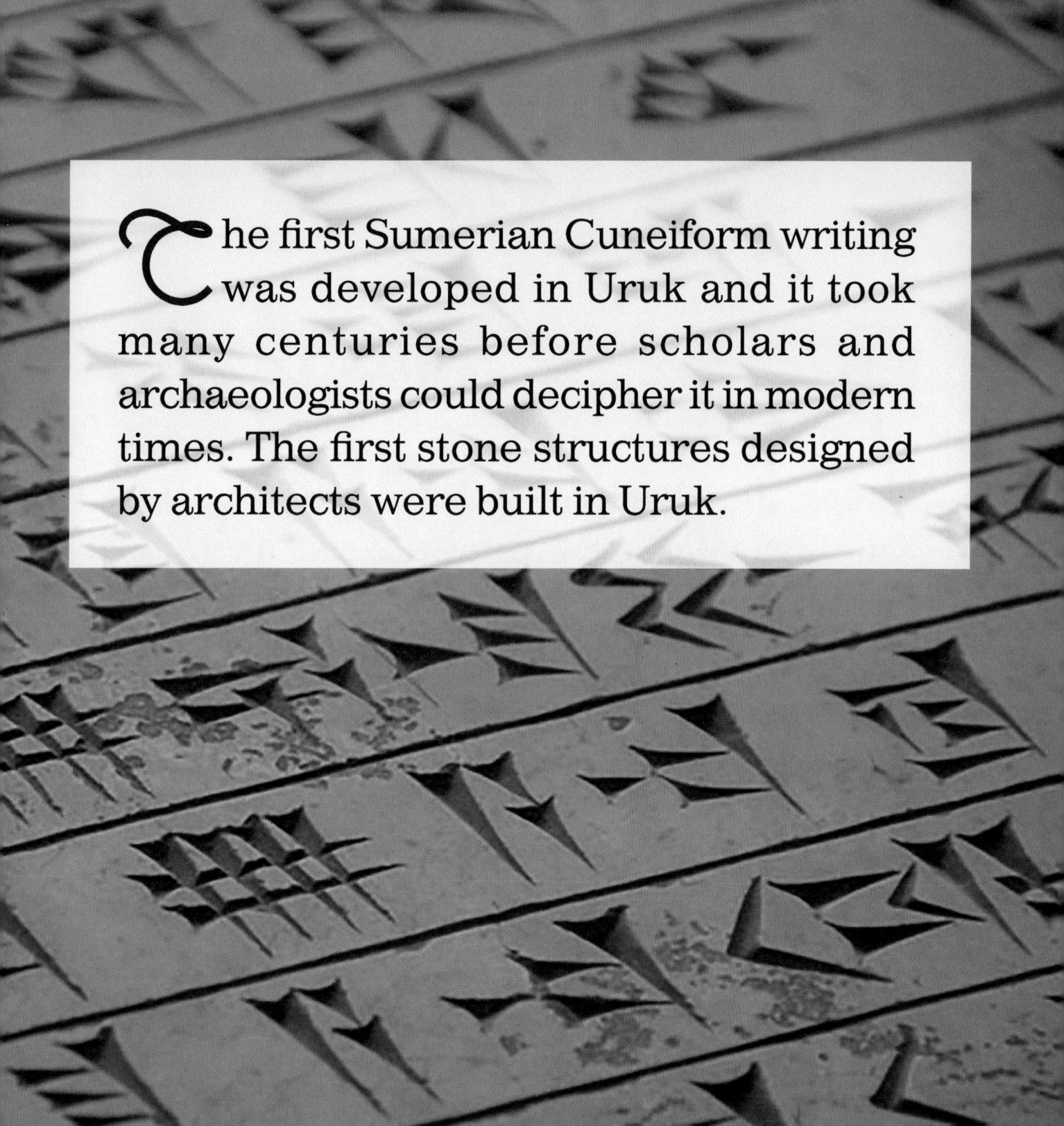

The first Sumerian Cuneiform writing was developed in Uruk and it took many centuries before scholars and archaeologists could decipher it in modern times. The first stone structures designed by architects were built in Uruk.

They were also the first to create and use a cylinder seal. The cylinder seal was essentially an engraving on stone that was created by an artist. The seal was like an individual's story told in art and was used to authenticate that person's identity. Similar to today, if you need to sign a legal document, you would write your signature on it.

Cylinder Seal

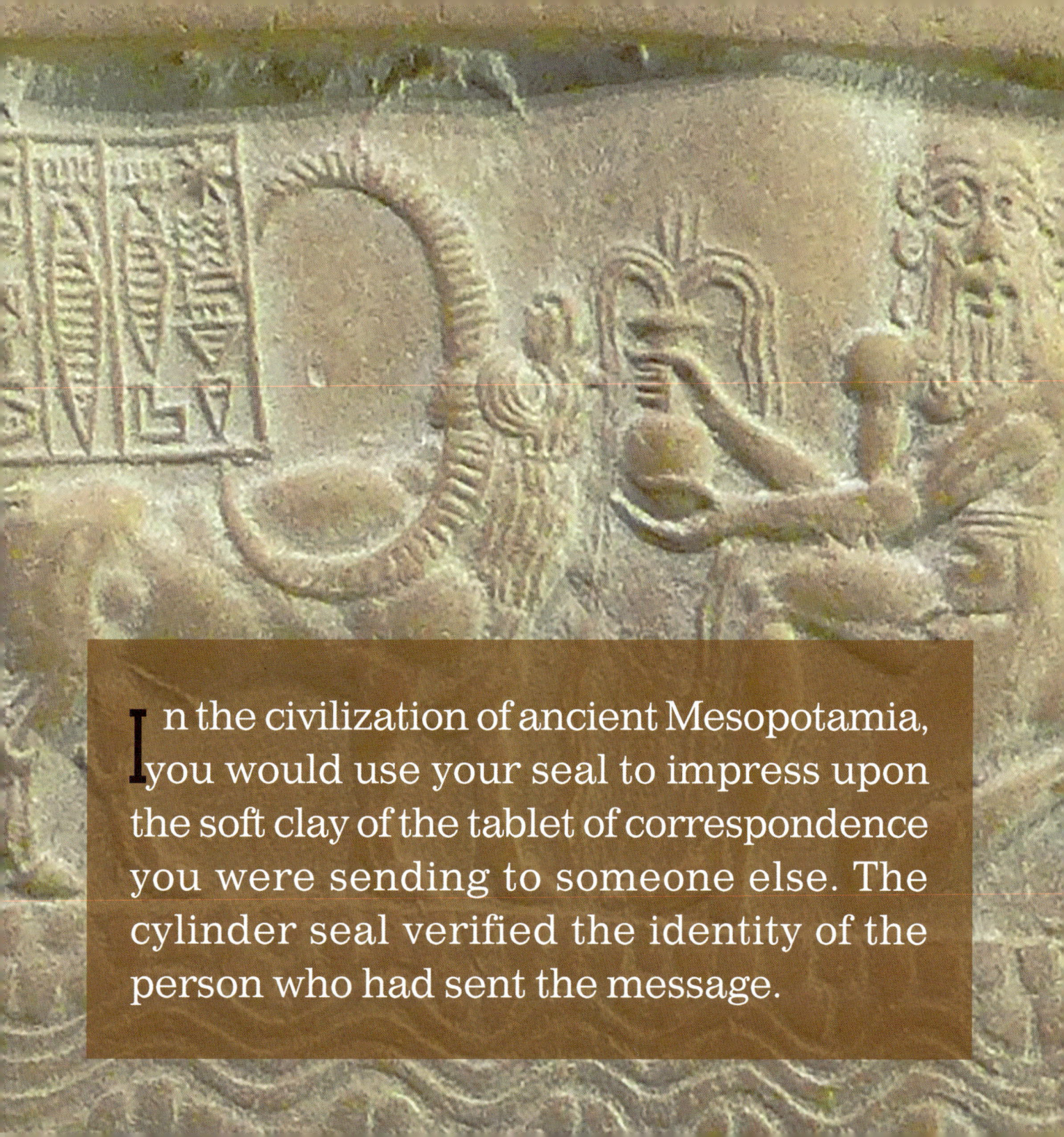

In the civilization of ancient Mesopotamia, you would use your seal to impress upon the soft clay of the tablet of correspondence you were sending to someone else. The cylinder seal verified the identity of the person who had sent the message.

AKKAD

The Empire of Akkadian is considered to be the first empire ever established. Akkad was the dominant city of the empire. The powerful leader Sargon the Great had a strong military and he conquered a large number of the city-states of Sumeria and ultimately controlled the civilization of Mesopotamia.

Akkadians

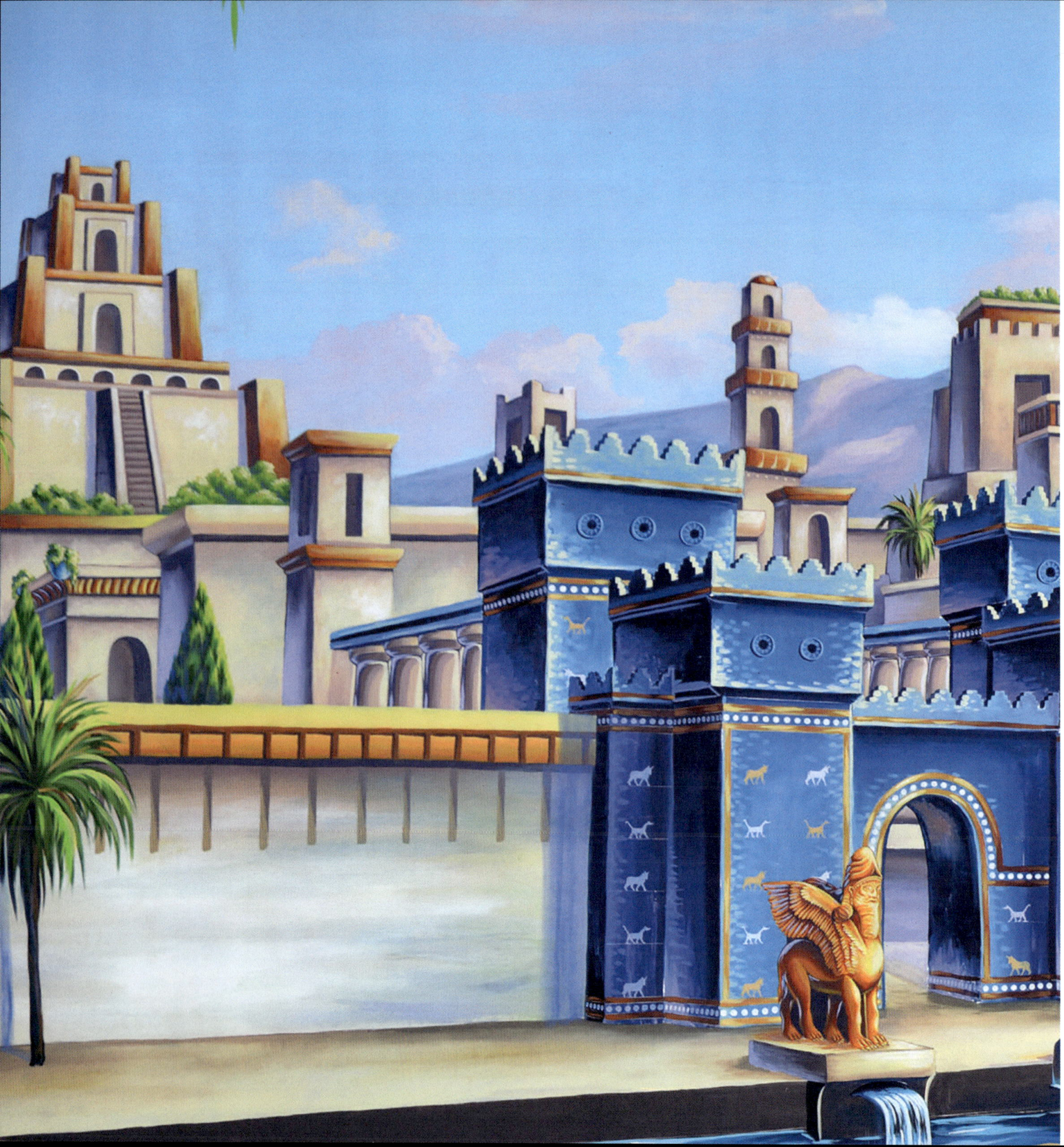

The language spoken by the Akkadians gradually took the place of the Sumerian language. It continued as the dominant language during the reign of the empire of Babylon as well as Assyria.

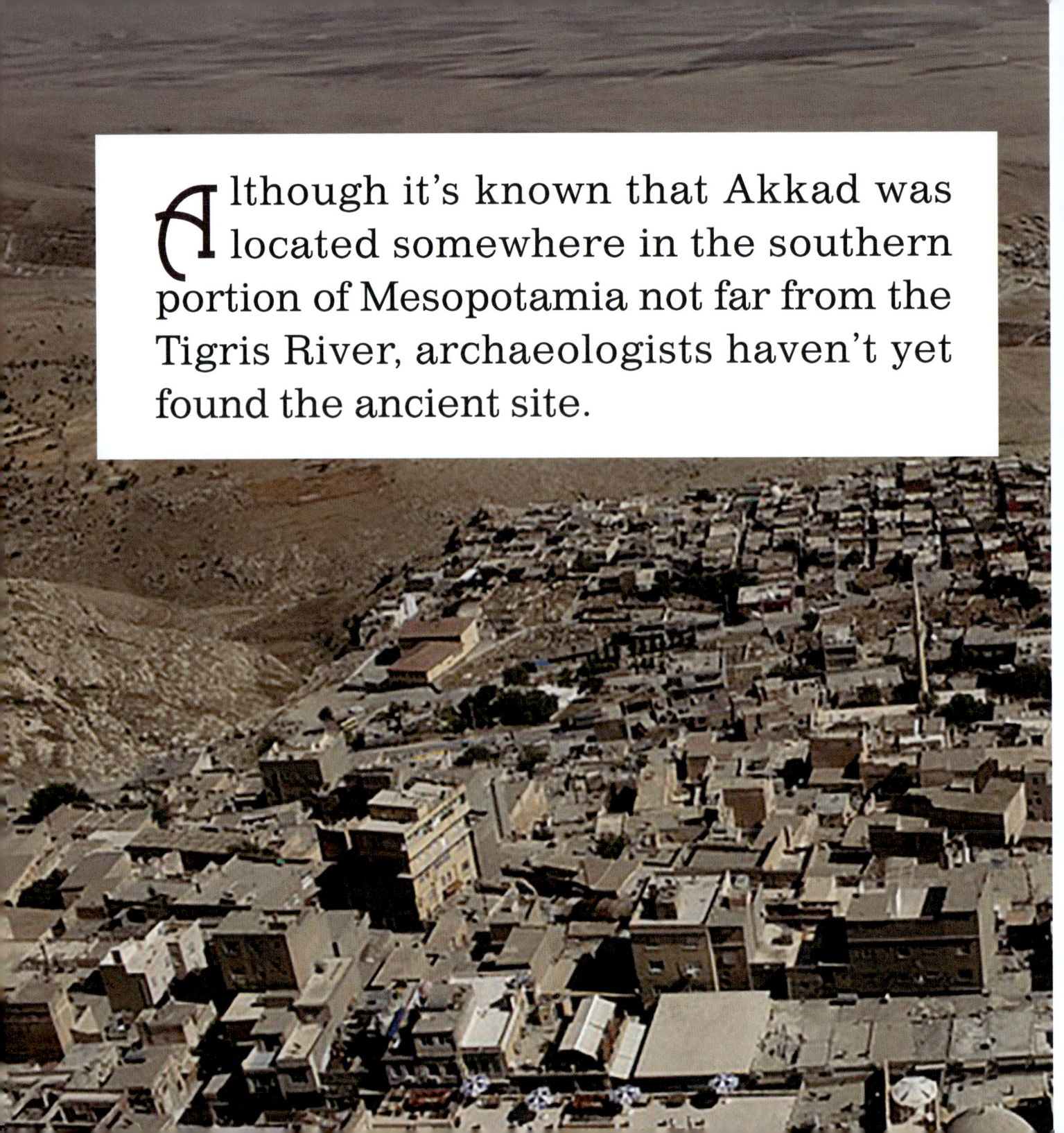

Although it's known that Akkad was located somewhere in the southern portion of Mesopotamia not far from the Tigris River, archaeologists haven't yet found the ancient site.

Mardin City

Ashur

ASHUR

The city of Ashur, also known as Assur, was named after the most important god worshipped by the Assyrians. Ashur was the first capital of the Empire of Assyria. As time went on, the capital city was moved to other locations. However, the city of Ashur was still considered to be the spiritual and religious hub of the empire.

BABYLON

The capital and central hub of the Empire of Babylonia, the city of Babylon, was once the most populated city in the world. Over 200,000 citizens lived there. The great king, Hammurabi, who created one of the first collections of strict laws, ruled the Empire from 1792 through 1750 BC.

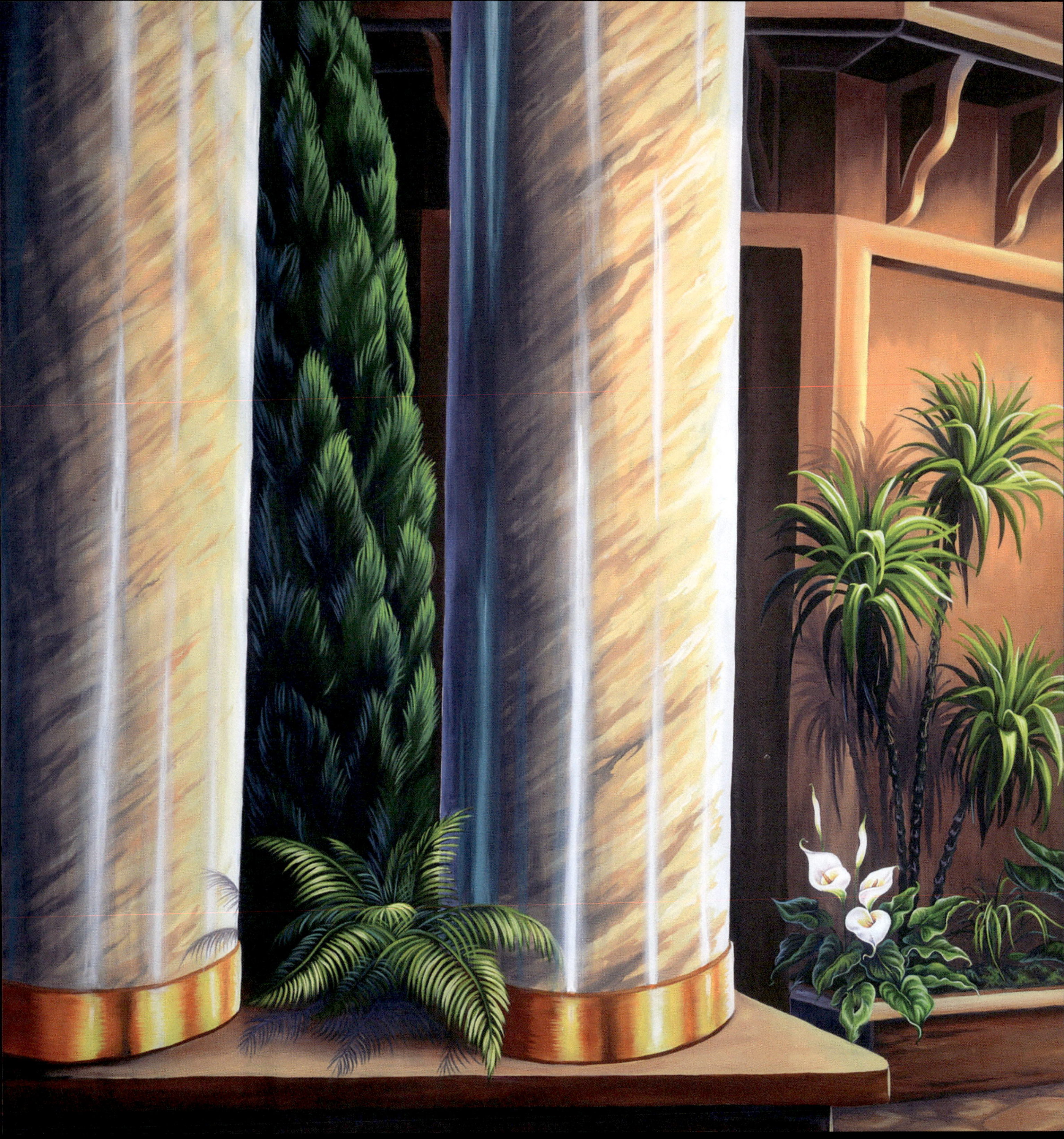

The Hanging Garden

Later in Babylon's history, King Nebuchadnezzar who ruled from 605 BC to 562 BC, had the Hanging Gardens constructed. His wife, Amyitis, came from green, lush lands with mountains and she was depressed in the flat, arid desert.

The king built the pyramid-like structure with garden terraces to lift her depression. The gardens were written about centuries later and proclaimed one of the Seven Wonders of the Ancient

World, but their ruins have never been found.

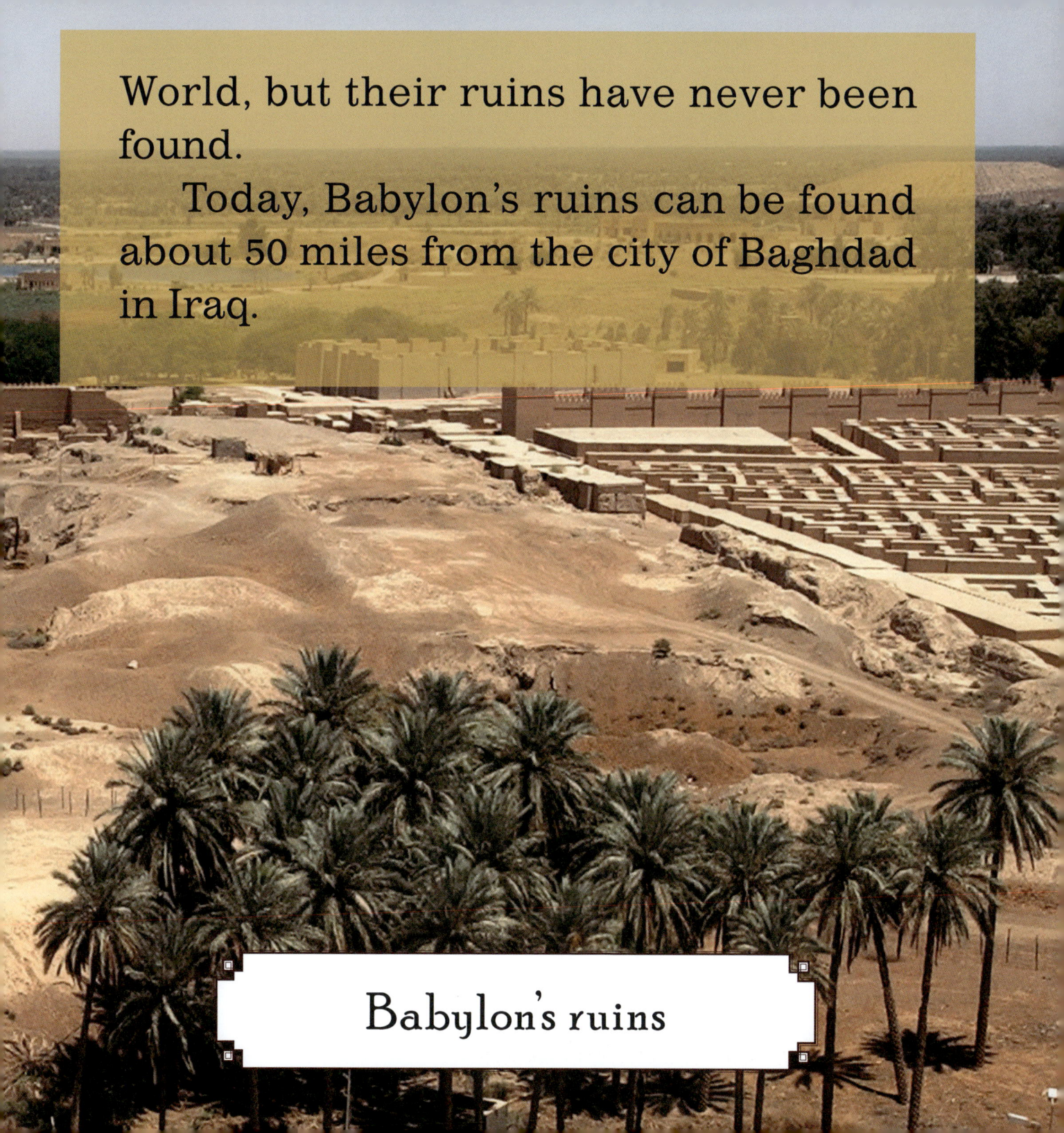

Today, Babylon's ruins can be found about 50 miles from the city of Baghdad in Iraq.

Babylon's ruins

Stele of Amenhotep

NIMRUD

The city of Nimrud became famous when King Ashurnasirpal II decided to locate the capital of the Assyrian Empire there. He rebuilt the city with an enormous palace and beautiful temples. There was a grand opening ceremony in 879 BC with a banquet serving many guests. A huge stone slab, called a stele, was found by archaeologists at the site. It described the festive events in detail.

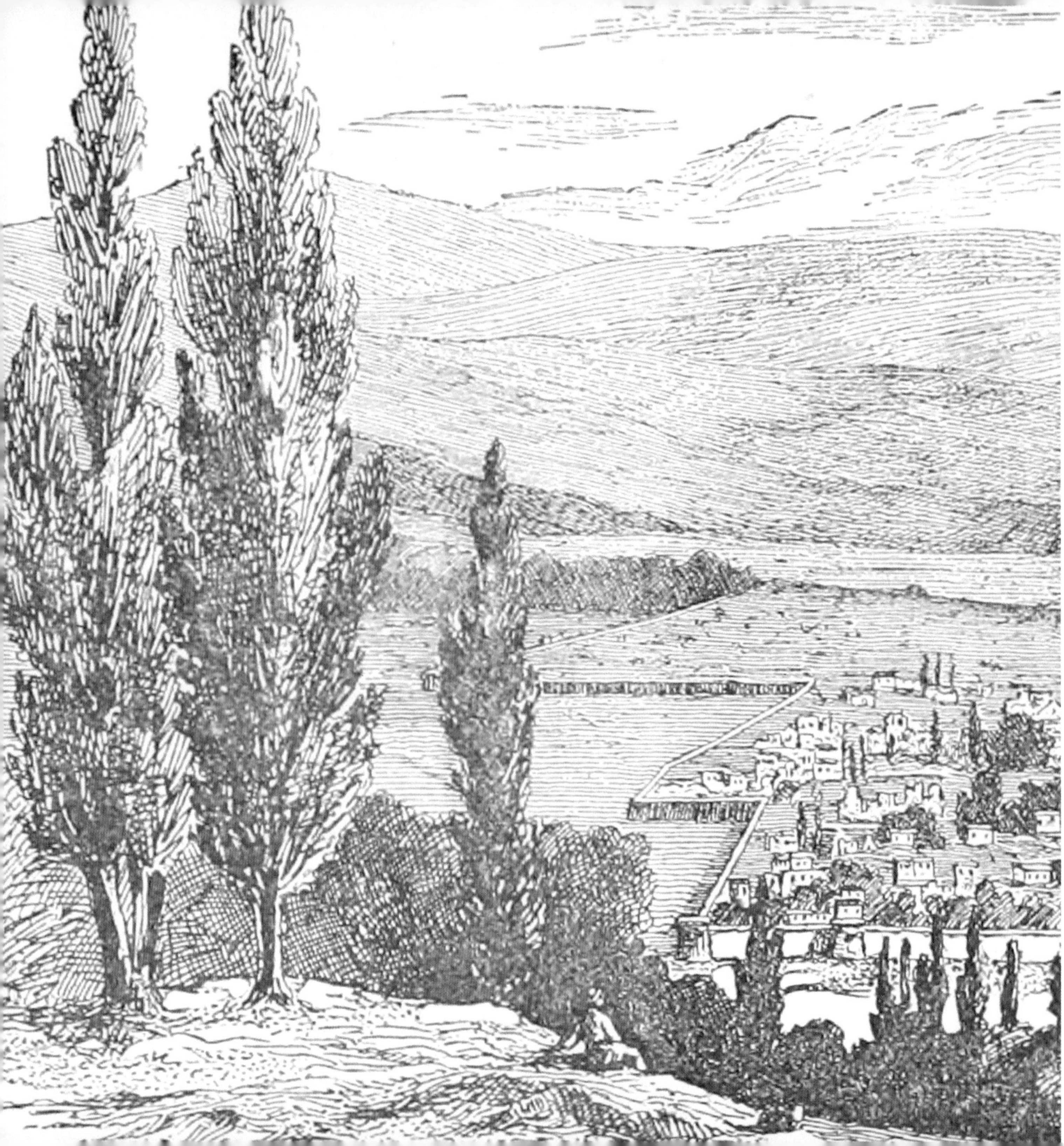

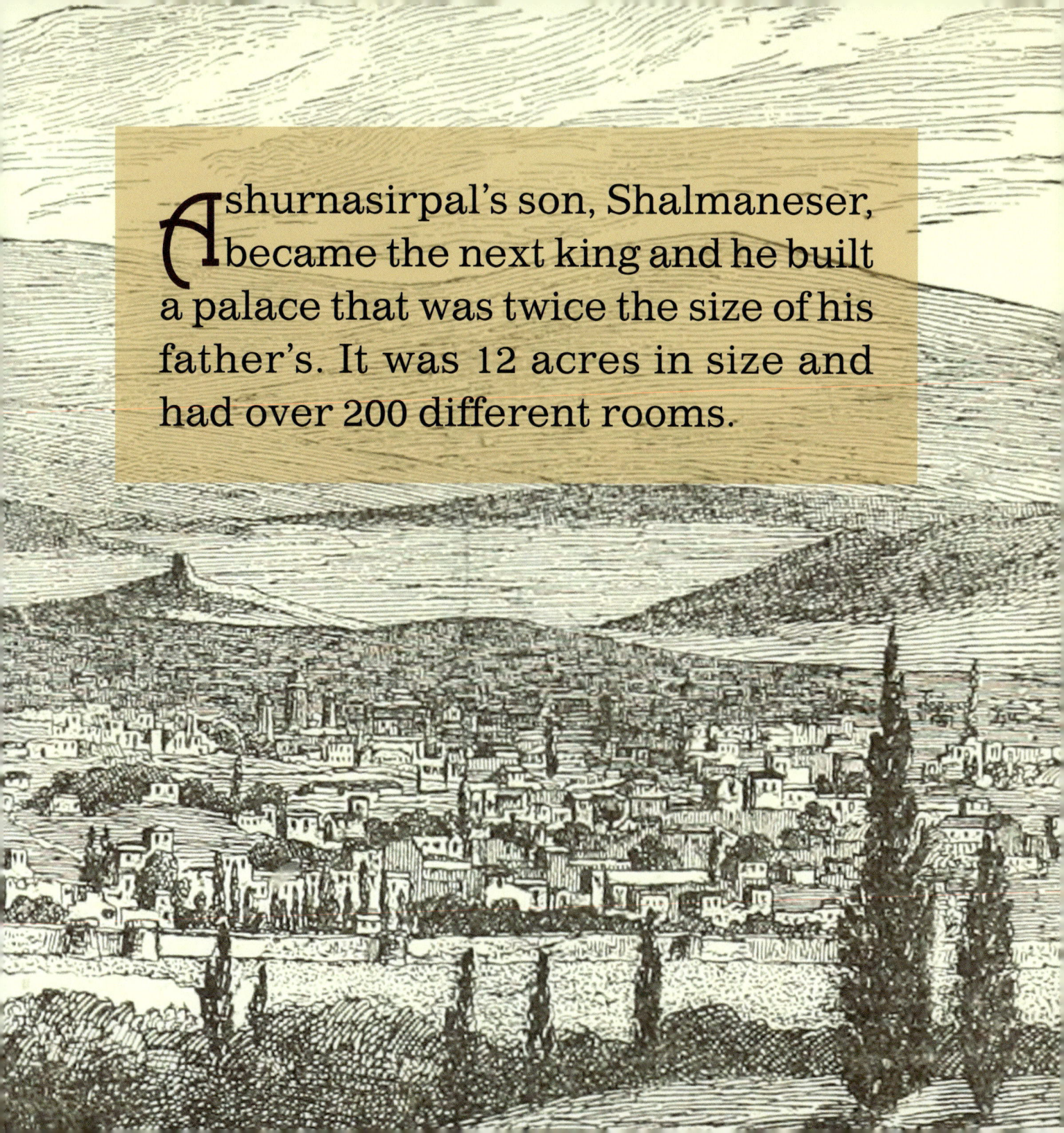

Ashurnasirpal's son, Shalmaneser, became the next king and he built a palace that was twice the size of his father's. It was 12 acres in size and had over 200 different rooms.

Nineveh Ruins

NINEVEH

At the peak of Assyrian civilization, Ninevah was the most populated city. It was constructed under the leadership of King Sennacherib around the year 700 Bc. The city was surrounded by walls that covered a 7 square kilometer region of land. There were 15 gates and 18 canals bringing water to different sections within the city.

The last powerful king of the Empire of Assyria was King Ashurbanipal. He was kind and just to his people but incredibly cruel to his enemies. He constructed a great library in Ninevah that contained 20,000 tablets. These tablets have provided the information we have today about these great past civilizations.

In the Bible, God asked Jonah to warn the people of Ninevah of their evil ways. However, Jonah is afraid to go and God has a whale swallow him. Once Jonah repents, the whale coughs him up and he goes forward to warn the people of Ninevah of God's wrath.

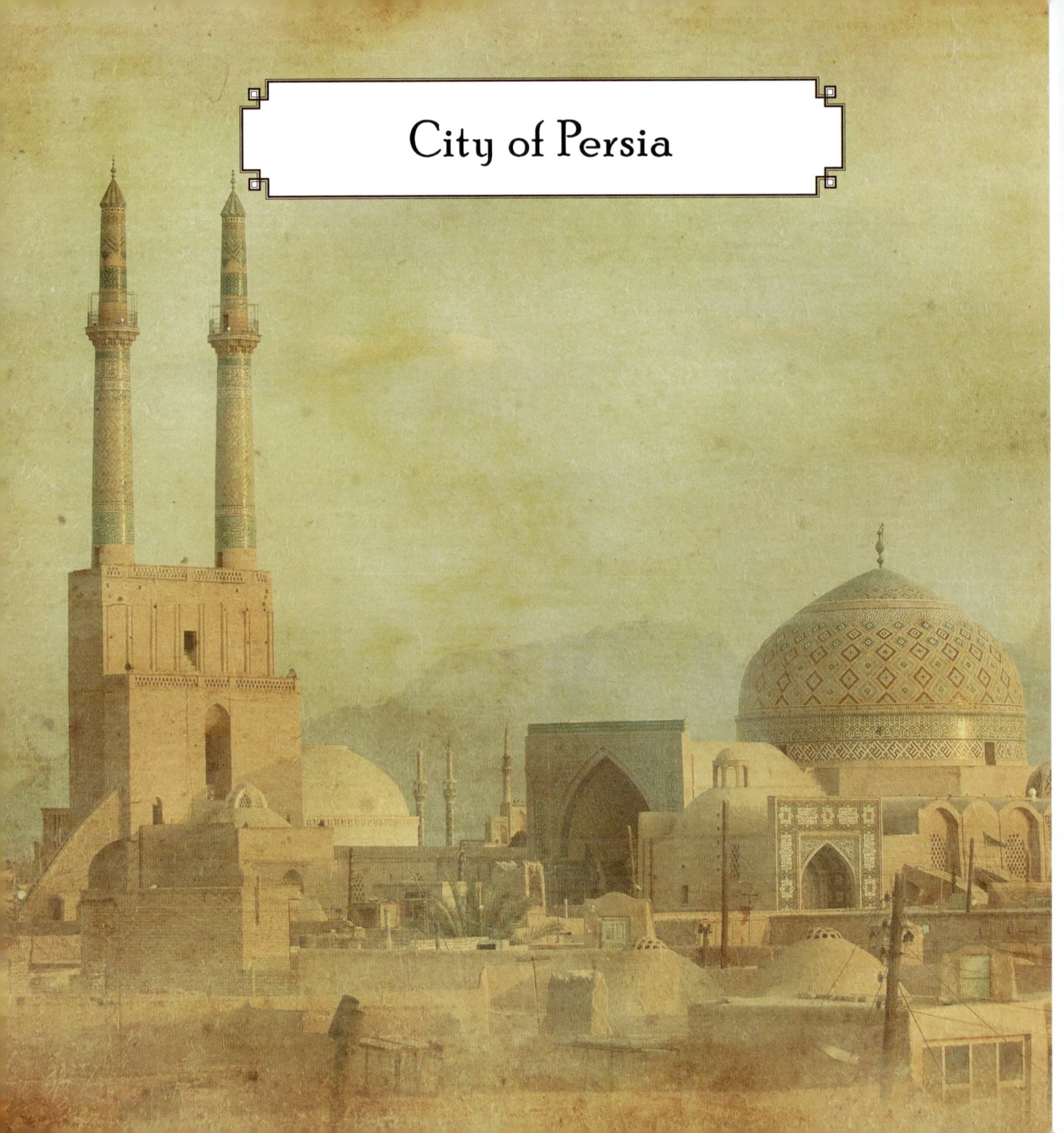

City of Persia

PERSEPOLIS

In the Greek language, Persepolis translates to "city of Persia." Currently, archaeologists are reconstructing some of the city's greatest landmarks, such as the Gate of Nations as well as the Apadana Palace. Persepolis was the Persian Empire's capital city, originally constructed about 515 Bc by Cyrus the Great.

Map: Mesopotamia and surrounding region, showing Lake Van, Lake Urmia, Tabriz, Qezel Owzan, Aleppo, Mosul, Asadābād Pass, Damascus, Baghdad, Syria, Iraq, Syrian Desert, Euphrates, Tigris, Khābūr, Diyala, Karkheh, Tharthār Depression, Bahr al Milh, Jabal 'Unayzah, Şahrā' al Hijārah, Hawr al Hammār, Wadi as Sirhān, Amman, Neutral Zone. Elevations: 5643, 4180, 13675, 10190, 1385, 11073, 5905, 3068, 3510, 2329, 1212.

Awesome! Now you know more about the ancient cities of the civilization of Mesopotamia. You can find more Ancient History books from Baby Professor by searching the website of your favorite book retailer.

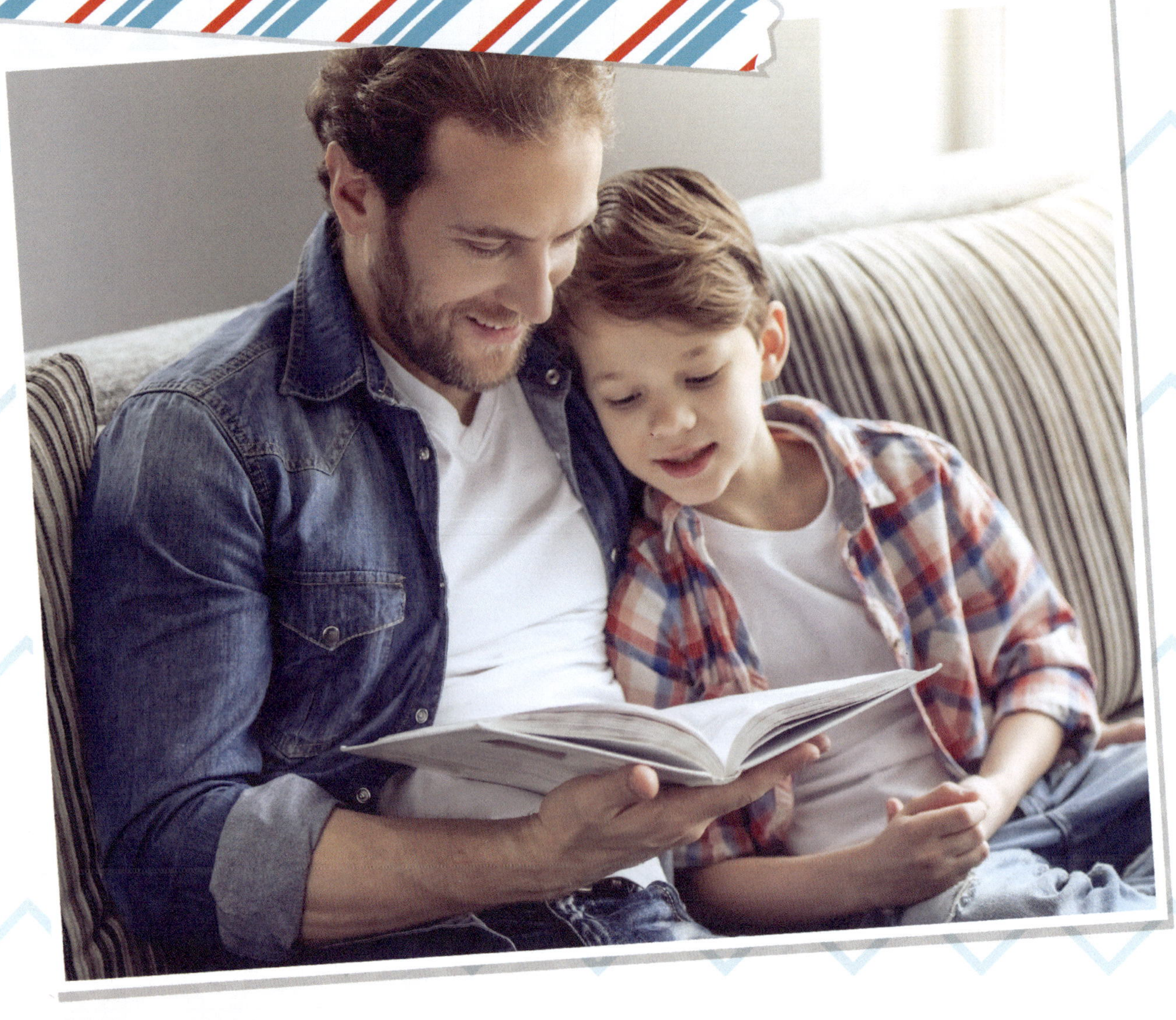

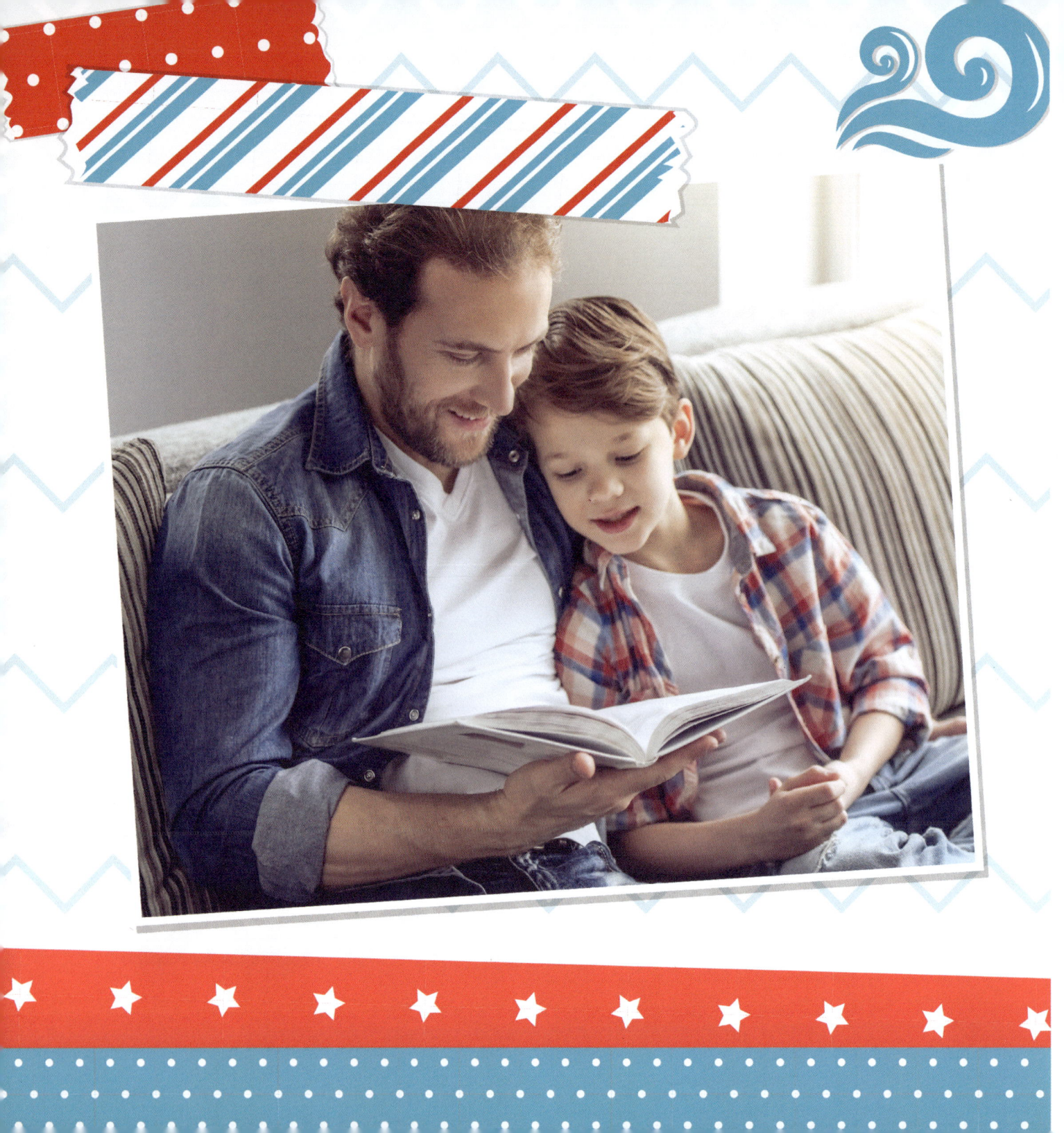

Visit

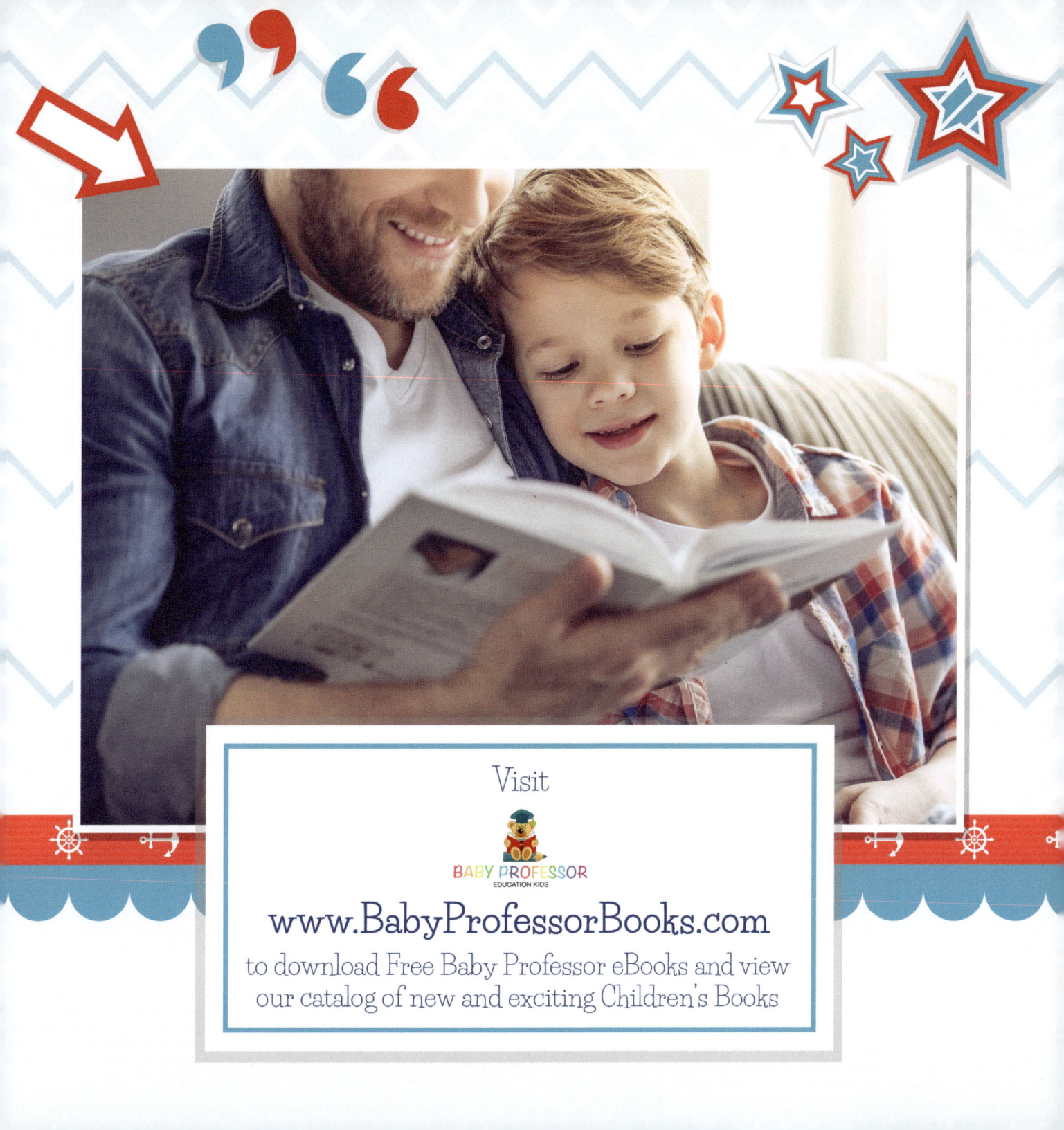

BABY PROFESSOR
EDUCATION KIDS

www.BabyProfessorBooks.com

to download Free Baby Professor eBooks and view our catalog of new and exciting Children's Books

Printed in Great Britain
by Amazon